Introduction

What is Google App Script?

Well -according to Google:
'*Google Apps Script is a scripting language based on JavaScript that lets you do new and cool things with Google Apps like Docs, Sheets, and Forms*'.
Of course that is absolutely true. But Google App Script is also a fantastic opportunity to learn programming -because all it takes is a device, an internet connection and a free Google account.

Google App Script (we are going to start calling it GAS) is the computer programming environment linked to Google Sheets and Google Docs. GAS is based on Javascript, with the addition of special functions that allow you to interact with Docs and Sheets. All scripts are run on Google's servers and stored on the cloud. Because everything is stored on the cloud you can write your own programs and games without downloading any software or needing a fancy device. You can start your program at home on the family computer, add to it at the public library and then run it for your friends on their phones or tablets - all without having to move your files around.

This screenshots in this book are from Google's Chrome browser, but any browser will do. It doesn't matter if you are using a desktop, laptop or tablet and the operating system isn't important. Because GAS runs on Google servers all you need is somewhere to type your code. The downside of this is that if you are on a very slow internet connection you may have to wait a few seconds for your code to run – just be patient.

Who is the book meant for?

Anybody who wants to learn to program. It happens to be written to take advantage of the GAS environment, but it is primarily an introduction to programming and not designed to make you an expert in GAS in particular. No programming knowledge is assumed and initially, every single step is explained.

This book was written with kids in mind, but is a good introductory text for any beginner. The goal of this book is to take someone who has never written a single line of code and make them confident enough to write a short program and knowledgeable enough to keep learning independently.

What do you need?

An internet-connected device (preferably something with an easy to use keyboard). A Google account. That's it. If you don't have a Google account you can sign up for free.

What's in this book?

We start off by playing a simple math game, then we look at the code behind it. Every step of the math game will be carefully explained. Along the way we are going to learn some coding basics, like how to work with strings and numbers, and how to use special statements like `if...else` and `while`.

Instead of starting with general coding concepts this book aims to teach through example. You will jump right into writing your first program. The set-up may seem a little repetitive, but that's to help to learn and become more familiar with the GAS environment.

By the time you have worked through this project you should feel comfortable reading basic Javascript and have the skills to learn the three projects on the website for this book https://sites.google.com/site/gascoding . One is an encryption program, this one is fun to write (and use) with a friend. The second is an automatic paragraph writer for those of you who don't like writing your own stories. In the last project you start to interact a little more with Google Sheets with a tic-tac-toe game.

Before you start

You need to have a Google account. If you don't have one already, go to the Google home page and click on the **Sign in** button at the top right of the screen.
Enter your email and choose a password and you're ready to get started!

A Critical Skill: Copying and Pasting

You also need to know how to copy and paste text. How you do this depends on what type of device you are using.

On **Windows:**
Press the `Ctrl` and `C` buttons to copy and `Ctrl` and `V` to paste

On **Mac**:
Press the ⌘ and `C` buttons to copy and ⌘ and `V` to paste

Our Project: A simple math game

We are going to begin at the end. First you are going to play the game a couple of times and get a feel for what it does and then we will figure out how to write the program behind the game. I'm going to assume that you've never used a Google script before, so we will walk slowly through each step, taking breaks to learn about coding as we go. Before we play the game, we need to get the game. It involves a few steps, but we'll walk through them slowly.

Setting Things Up

Step 1: Open a new Google Sheet

To do this open Google Drive, click the red New button on the left hand side of the screen and select Google Sheets. You should see a screen like this:

Click on the words *Untitled spreadsheet* and type a name. I called mine Math Game.

This is the Google Sheet that your game will run from. Each program script you write will be 'behind' either a Google Sheet or a Google Doc.

Step 2: **Open the Programming Screen**

To code in Google Docs or Google Sheets you need to open the Script Editor. This is where you are going to write all your code.

Open the Script Editor

Click on Tools > Script Editor.

Click on Blank Project

Select Blank Project underneath *Create Script For*

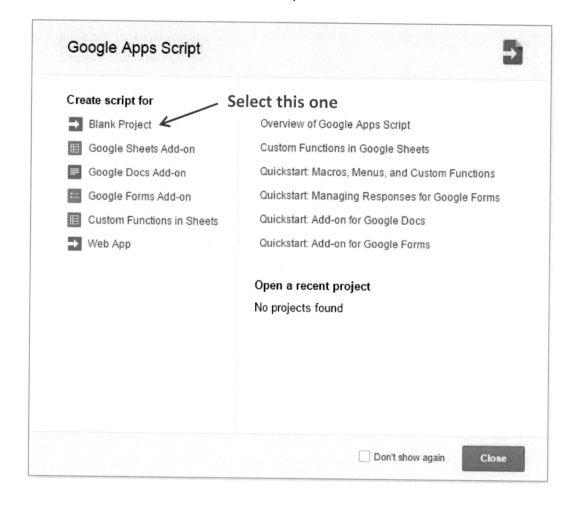

This is what the Script Editor looks like

Give your project a name

I called mine Math Game (double click on *Untitled project* to do this)

Delete everything in Code.gs

Select all text and hit delete. We are going to replace it with the code for the math program.

Step 3: Get the game.

Copy the Math Game Code from the Learn Coding With Google site by following these steps:

1. In your web browser open a new tab and go to the website https://sites.google.com/site/gascoding/ . This contains all the code for the game.

2. Copy all the text under Code For Math Game.

3. Go back to your programming screen from Step 2.

4. Paste the code you copied into Code.gs

5. Save the program.

Your screen should look like this:

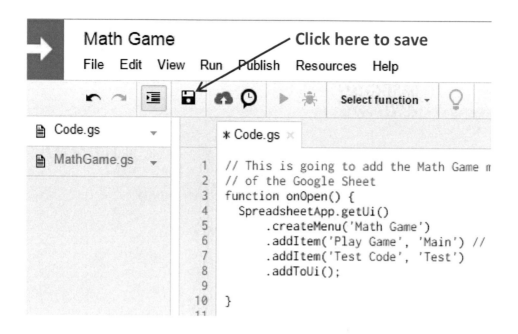

Math Game

— Click here to save

File   Edit   View   Run   Publish   Resources   Help

Select function ▾

Code.gs

MathGame.gs

* Code.gs ×

```
1   // This is going to add the Math Game m
2   // of the Google Sheet
3   function onOpen() {
4     SpreadsheetApp.getUi()
5         .createMenu('Math Game')
6         .addItem('Play Game', 'Main') //
7         .addItem('Test Code', 'Test')
8         .addToUi();
9
10  }
11
```

SUMMARY

You have opened up a new Google Sheet. You've opened the Script Editor and pasted all the code for the game into it. Ideally you should have two tabs open on your web browser - one for the sheet and one for the code.

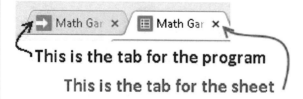

Math Gar ×   Math Gar ×

This is the tab for the program

This is the tab for the sheet

If you accidentally closed the code screen then just select Tools > Script Editor from the Sheet screen.

Playing the Game

Click on a button that looks like this ↻ . This button is usually to the left of the address bar in your web browser.

Play the Math Game

Once your sheet has refreshed you should see a new menu called Math Game at the top of the screen to the right of Help. Click on that and then select Play Game.

Play the game again

I'm guessing since you are keen enough to be reading this book that when you were asked whether you wanted to do some easy multiplication you clicked Yes - so this time click No (or if you're already clicked No click Yes).

You should have a pretty good idea of what the program does. That is the important first step in learning how to program - deciding what the program should do!

Understanding the Game

Our goal is to write this math game. Before we can write a program though, we really need to have a good understanding of exactly what it does. We are going to *deconstruct* or break apart the program into small steps. Go get some paper and a pencil.

Write down a list of what happens in the game

Play the math game once more. This time write down a list of everything that happens –these are the things that you are going to learn how to program.

Here is my list:

1. Ask for the player's name.
2. Ask whether the player would like to do some easy multiplication.
3. Tell the player how many questions will be asked and how hard they will be.
4. Ask multiplication questions until there are five correct answers.
5. Tell the player that the game is over and how many questions it took to get five correct answers.

Coming up with this list is an important first step to programming. Before you start writing any code you need to decide exactly what your program needs to do. We are going to go through each of these five things in our list and learn how to program them using Google App Script.

Starting a New Project

Create a new Google Sheet

We are going to start coding from scratch, so open up a new Google Sheet and a new coding screen. This is very similar to what we have just done. Open a new Google Sheet and name it something - I called mine My Math Game. To give yours a name double-click on *Untitled Spreadsheet* at the top.

Open up a new programming screen.

1. Click on Tools > Script Editor.

2. Select Blank Project underneath *Create Script For*

3. Name your project. I called mine My Math Game.

4. Select and delete all the text in Code.gs, so that you just have a blank page.

This is what you should see

SUMMARY

You have played the Math Game a few times and written down a list of what it does. You have opened up a new Google Sheet and named it. You've opened the Script Editor and deleted all the code so that you have a blank script file to start coding into. Now you should have four tabs open on your web browser:

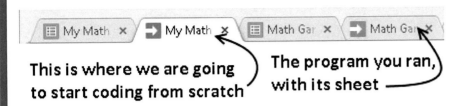

This is where we are going to start coding from scratch

The program you ran, with its sheet

We are ready to start coding!

Creating a Menu with the onOpen Function

The onOpen function is a special function in Google App Script. If a document or a spreadsheet has an onOpen function it will run whenever the document or spreadsheet file is opened. If you want your document or spreadsheet to have a menu then the onOpen function is where you put it. Our onOpen function adds a Menu, and two menu items to our Google Sheet.

Type this code into your blank script editor

```
1    function onOpen() {
2    SpreadsheetApp.getUi()
3    .createMenu('Math Game')
4    .addItem('Play Game', 'Main')
5    .addItem('Test Code', 'Test')
6    .addToUi();
7    }
```

> **Type Carefully!**
> Make sure that you have all your periods and CAPITALS in the right places.

Here's what is going on in each line of code, the green numbers match the green numbers in the above code:

1   We give our function a name, followed by **()** and start it with a brace **{**.

2   This line gets a reference to the user interface. If we were using a Google Doc we would type: `DocumentApp.getUI()`

3   This creates the menu and names it Math Game

4   This adds the menu item Play Game and links it to a function called Main.

5   The adds the menu item Test Code and links it to a function called Test.

6   This adds the entire menu to the user's sheet. Because this is the end of the instruction we put a semicolon at the end.

7   We always need to close our function with a brace **}**

Make sure you use the right quotes

The correct quote marks to use are the single quotes. This key if usually two keys to the right of the 'L' on a keyboard. If you are using the correct quotes then all of the words between your quote marks will show up in red on the screen.

Refresh your Google Sheet

Now, go back to your Google Sheet (green tab called My Math Game) and refresh the page (using this ↻) you will see a new menu called Math Game. If you click on Math Game there will be two items: Play Game and Test Code. Don't click them - you will get an error because we haven't written any code to go with those items yet.

Getting An Error

Actually - Go ahead and click on one of your new menu items

You will get this error:

Script function not found: Main **Details** **Dismiss**

The error is telling you that the function the menu item is linked to can't be found. Click Dismiss on the error and it will go away. The reason that the function can't be found is that ... you haven't written it yet!

Programmers get lots and lots of errors. Don't worry, there is usually a simple reason for it...even if you can't figure out what it is right away. Errors are known as bugs in programming. Often bugs are caused by a typing mistake. If you are struggling through this example, remember that you have all the source code for the game on the *Learn Coding With Google* website and if you need to you can copy and paste from the source code into your coding screen.

Coding the game: An attack plan

We know that our program needs to perform five basic tasks. Even with a short program like this there is room for mistakes. Computers don't have brains - they don't know that you meant to write `function` when you really wrote `fncution` - so they will just give you an error.

The Google App Script (GAS) programming environment is actually pretty good - it can usually tell you where your error is. We want to be on the safe side though so we are going to do a little of the program in a special Test function and once we have that bit working we are going to move it to the Main function.

Add the following code to your Code.gs script:

```
// This is our test function
function Test(){
}

// This is our main function
function Main(){
}
```

Brackets, Braces and Parentheses

( )	**Parentheses** are used when defining functions and calling functions
{ }	**Braces** (sometimes called curly brackets) are used to define the start and end of a block of code.
[ ]	**Brackets** are used to identify elements of an array. Arrays won't be covered in this project .

Type Carefully!

It is important that you type the function names exactly as they appear in the onOpen function. The onOpen function links menu items to functions in your script. If the functions aren't typed the same way in both the onOpen function and later in the their own function names then you will get an error.

Javascript Syntax

Javascript isn't a tough language to learn – but it does have its rules. Here are a few basic ones:

Capitalisation matters
The variable myName is NOT the same as myname.

Braces are important
All the code for a function must be between the two braces { and }.

Don't forget the semi-colon
End each command with a semi-colon ;

Use quotes consistently
Use either single quotes ' or double quotes " to put text in, but be consistent.

Here's what you should have so far:

```
// This is going to add the Math Game menu to the top
// of the Google Sheet
function onOpen() {
  SpreadsheetApp.getUi()
      .createMenu('Math Game')
      .addItem('Play Game', 'Main')
      .addItem('Test Code', 'Test')
      .addToUi();

}

function Test(){
}

function Main(){
}
```

The function names must match the names in the addItem method

You'll notice when you type the red lines they show up in red on the screen. That is because these are comment lines. They are not part of your program and the computer doesn't try to read them. They are notes to you, the programmer, so that you remember why you wrote something.

It is good practice to get into the habit of commenting your code. It will make changing your program and finding bugs in your program much easier.

SUMMARY

You have already put three functions into your code file – the Code.gs script file. The first function is the onOpen function that will run every time your Google Sheet is opened. In this function you instructed the Google servers to add a new menu, with two menu items to your Google Sheet. The next two functions, Test and Main are empty functions – they don't do anything yet. At this point you should be able to see your new menu called Math Game on your Google sheet and click on either item without getting an error. Clicking on the items won't do anything yet – because your functions are empty, but you shouldn't get any errors either.

Comments

Comments are not code – they just regular writing around code.
Comments start with two forward slashes (//). Whatever you type after the comment marks won't be read as computer code. Programmers write comments into their programs as notes to themselves and other programmers. Comments are there to help the programmer understand what the code is meant to do. The comments above the onOpen function explain what the onOpen function is going to do.

All programming languages have comments. In Google App Script there are two ways to write comments. You can write a comment after typing // or, you can put a comment between /* and */. Comments that start with // finish on the same line. Comments between /* and */ can be as many lines long as you would like.

Examples of Comments

// This is a one line comment

var myName = 'Bob'; // This is a comment after some code

/* Or you can write a comment like this. It can
be as long as you like.
It just has to start with the forward slash and asterisk and finish with an asterisk and forward slash.*/

Using prompts to ask the player a question

The first thing our program should do is ask the player their name.

To do this we are going to use the **prompt** method. For now, we are going to write our code in our Test function.

Code for Math Game Step 1

Type the following into your Test function:

```
function Test(){
 var ui = SpreadsheetApp.getUi();
 ui.prompt('Please enter your name.', ui.ButtonSet.OK);
}
```

Now your Test function has two *instructions*. The first instruction gets a reference to the user interface and stores it in a variable name **ui**. When working with Google App Script we almost always need this line of code in our program. By assigning the user interface to a variable we can show messages and ask the player questions.

The second line shows the player a prompt. A prompt has two parts: first the message you want to display and then the buttons you want to use.

Test it

Save your code, go back to your sheet and from the Math Game menu select Test Code.

Now you should see this:

Congratulations! You have written a working program!

You made that prompt appear using this line of code:

```
ui.prompt('What is your name?', ui.ButtonSet.OK);
```

The text in red is the message you want to show the player. It will show up in red on your screen to tell you that you have typed text and variables (more on that in a little while).

You called the prompt method for the user interface and provided two bits of information:
1. The prompt text ('What is your name?')
2. The buttons we wanted to show (ui.ButtonSet.OK) (see the green box below)

Try changing the prompt so that it asks for the player's age instead of their name. Then change it back and we'll move on to step 2.

Going back to our list of five things that our program should do our second item was: *Ask whether the player would like to do some easy multiplication.*

The second question looked like this:

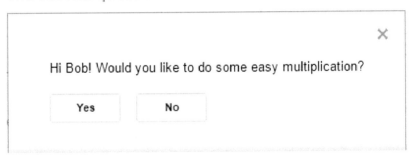

This looks pretty similar to the first step - we present the player with a question. Except now we need to put the player's name into the question. This part of the program is going to need to change, based on what the player told us their name was in Step 1. To do that, we need to store the user's name from the first prompt in a *variable*.

Google Button Sets

There are four types of button sets to choose from:
OK   OK_CANCEL   YES_NO   YES_NO_CANCEL

Change the second line to look like this:

Go back into the script editor.

```
var response = ui.prompt('What is your name?', ui.ButtonSet.OK);
```

This saves what the player typed into a variable called *response*.

We aren't quite ready to use it though. We need to get a particular *property* of the response that stores the text that the player entered.

Underneath the last line type this:

```
var student = response.getResponseText();
```

This stores the text that the player entered into the variable student.

Let's have another look at the second question:

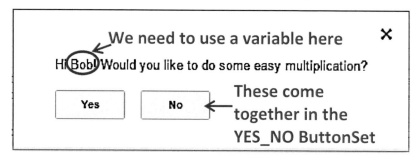

Did you notice anything different about this prompt compared to the first one? There is no place for the player to type anything, no *textbox*.
The command to present this type of information to the player is called an *alert*. The *alert* method doesn't show the user a text box. That's the difference between the alert method and the prompt method.

To make this screen appear we need to use an alert command, we need to include the player's name in the message and we need to tell the computer to show the Yes and No buttons.

Code for Math Game Step 2

Type the following into your script:

```
var response = ui.alert('Hi' + student +
    ' Would you like to do some easy multiplication?',
    ui.ButtonSet_YES_NO)
```

Your complete code should look like this:

```
// This is going to add the Math Game menu to the top
// of the Google Sheet
function onOpen() {
 SpreadsheetApp.getUi()
     .createMenu('Math Game')
     .addItem('Play Game', 'Main')
     .addItem('Test Code', 'Test')
     .addToUi();
}

// This is our test function
function Test(){

// Step 1:
 var ui = SpreadsheetApp.getUi();
 var response = ui.prompt('Please enter your name.',
ui.ButtonSet.OK);
 var student = response.getResponseText();

// Step 2:
var response2 = ui.alert( 'Hi '+ student +
'! Would you like to do some easy multiplication?',
ui.ButtonSet.YES_NO);
}
```

This is all the code for Steps 1 and 2 of the Math Game. Now let's see how it looks from a player's perspective - and make sure it works like we expect it to.

Variable Types

A variable is a place where we can store something that we want to use later.

There are three types of basic variables in JavaScript and a couple of more complex types.

The three basic types of variables are: Number, String and Boolean
Here are some examples:

```
var pi = 3.14;        // Number
var pie = 'Apple';    // String
var likePie = true;   // Boolean
```

Numbers and Strings are pretty straightforward. Boolean variables can only take on one of two values - true or false

The other types of variables are Arrays and Objects. We won't use those in our first project, but here are some examples:

```
var pies = ['apple', 'raspberry', 'blueberry'];
var fruit = {name: 'banana', colour: 'yellow'};
```

Variable typing isn't strict in JavaScript like it is in some other languages. This mean that to declare a variable you just need to put var in front of it. You don't need to tell Javascript what *type* of variable it is.

You can use variables in your code wherever you would use numbers or text.

Example

When we write:
```
var student = 'Bob';
'Hi ' + student    would give us 'Hi Bob'
```
It's pretty easy to put text together in JavaScript -But be careful! Computers aren't smart - they can't spell.

So if you have:
```
var greeting = 'Hi'
```
Then: `greeting + student = 'HiBob'`
If you want spaces in your text you need to remember to put them in!

Test your program

From your Google Sheet Click on Math Game > Test Code

You should see this screen:

Then, if your name is Bob, this screen:

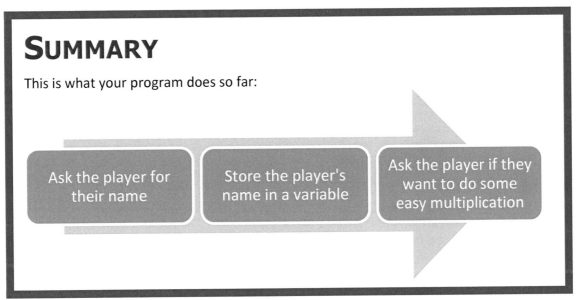

SUMMARY

This is what your program does so far:

- Ask the player for their name
- Store the player's name in a variable
- Ask the player if they want to do some easy multiplication

Before we move on we are going to copy the code from our Test function into our Main function. The Main function is where we are going to put our code once we know it is working properly.

Copy your code from Test to Main

Copy all the text between the braces { } in Test function and paste it between the braces in the Main function.

Your complete code should look like this:

```
// This is going to add the Math Game menu to the top
// of the Google Sheet
function onOpen() {
  SpreadsheetApp.getUi()
      .createMenu('Math Game')
      .addItem('Play Game', 'Main')
      .addItem('Test Code', 'Test')
      .addToUi();
}

function Test(){
// Step 1:
  var ui = SpreadsheetApp.getUi();
  var response = ui.prompt('Please enter your name.', ui.ButtonSet.OK);
  var student = response.getResponseText();

// Step 2:
var response2 = ui.alert( 'Hi '+ student +
'! Would you like to do some easy multiplication?',
ui.ButtonSet.YES_NO);
}

function Main(){
// Step 1:
  var ui = SpreadsheetApp.getUi();
  var response = ui.prompt('Please enter your name.', ui.ButtonSet.OK);
  var student = response.getResponseText();

// Step 2:
var response2 = ui.alert( 'Hi '+ student +
'! Would you like to do some easy multiplication?',
ui.ButtonSet.YES_NO);
}
```

This is just a copy of function Test()

Save your code, go back to your Google sheet and from the Math Game menu click
Play Game. You should see your prompt, followed by your alert.

Step 3: Responding to difference choices

In Step 3 of the program you tell your player how many questions there are and how
hard they will be based on their answer in Step 2.

If the player answered Yes to the question then the next screen looks like this:

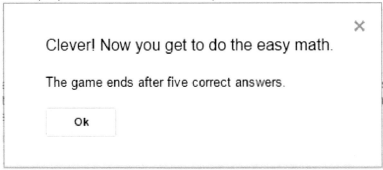

If the player answered No it looks like this:

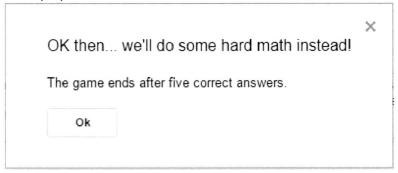

In Step 3 we need to tell our program to show one message if the user answered Yes,
and a different message if the user answered No.

We need to learn the if ...else statement!

If Else Statement

The If Else Statement is what is called a *conditional* statement. It allows you to run one bit of code if something is true, and a different bit of code if something is false.

In JavaScript the `if else` statement looks like this:

```
if (something) {
      run this bit of code if something is true
} else {
      run this bit of code if something is false
}
```

Braces are used to define which bits of code run if something is true and which bits of code to run if something is false. Google App Script makes it easy to see where matching braces are by highlighting pairs in green when you move over a brace with your cursor.

Examples

If else statements are pretty flexible:

You can use just the `if` part of the statement:

```
if (name == "Bob"){
var response = "That is a great name!";
}
```

Or you can use `if, else if ,else` statements to deal with more complex problems:

```
if (name == "Bob"){
var response = "That is a great name!";
} else if (name == "Sally") {
var response = "Wow -that's my mum's name!";
} else {
var response = "That is a boring name.";
}
```

Using the If Else Statement

In our program we are going to show one message if the user clicked Yes and another message if the user clicked No.

Look at your last line of code:

```
var response2 = ui.alert('Hi '+ student +
        '! Would you like to do some easy multiplication?',
ui.ButtonSet.YES_NO);
}
```

This will store the player's answer to the question in the variable *response2*.

We need to test if the response was the Yes button, so the first part of our if statement will look like this:

```
if (response2 == ui.Button.YES){
```

Hey – What is a double equal sign = = ?

A double equal sign is a *comparison operator*. It asks the question *are these two values (or variables) the same*? Comparison operators are used in program control statements like `if else` statements, `while` statements and `for` statements.

If you write this in your code:
```
if (response2 == ui.Button.YES){
        // all this code will be run if response2 was YES
}
```

You are testing if the variable `response` has the same value as ui.Button.YES – which is a value that indicates the user clicked the YES button on your alert. If the response is equal to ui.Button.YES then the code between the braces will be run. Otherwise, the program will continue to read the code after the closing brace, } and just pretend the code between the braces doesn't exist.

Assignments and Comparisons

Assignment operators assign values to variables.

These are examples of assignment operators:

```
var x = 1;
var y = 2;
var z = x + y;
```

Comparison operators test whether a statement is *true* or *false*.

Here are some examples with our x and y variables:

var x == y	asks if x is equal to y	false
var x < y	asks if x is less than y	true
var x <=	is x less than or equal to y	true
var x != y	is x not equal to y (tricky!)	true

So:

x = y assigns the value of x equal to the value of y

x == y tests whether or not x *is* equal to y

We need to use Comparison operators in if else statements.

Alerts and Prompts

By now, you are probably getting pretty comfortable with showing the user messages using the alert and prompt methods.

Let's take another look at what we want our message to look like:

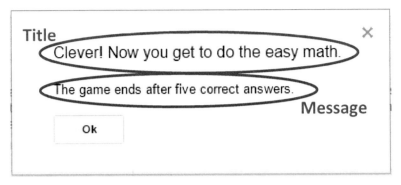

This is an alert, because there is no textbox. It uses the OK ButtonSet. You should be able to figure out how to do that - but hold on, it has TWO messages.

That's ok, the alert and prompt methods can both be used like this:

ui.alert(Title, Message, ButtonSet);

Up to this point we've been using them like this:

ui.alert(Message, ButtonSet); (without the Title)

But Google App Script will let you use either. It assumes if you provide three bits of information (called *arguments*) that you want the first one to be the title.

If the player responds No to the question, we will still show a message, but with different words in the Title and Message.

The other thing that we need to do based on the user's response is decide how hard the multiplication questions should be.

Cleaning up our Test Function

Before we put in the code for Step 3 we are going to clean up our Test function. We know that the code in the Test function works and we don't want to have to run the first part of our program to test the next part so we are going to get rid of the code in the Test function.

Delete all the code in your Test function

But don't delete the braces!

Code for Math Game Step 3

Type this into your Test function:

```
1    function Test(){
2    var ui = SpreadsheetApp.getUi(); // Always leave this line
3    var response2 = ui.Button.YES;
4    if (response2== ui.Button.YES){
5      var title= 'Clever! Now you get to do the easy math.';
6      var smallest=1;
7      var biggest=5;
8    } else {
9        var title = 'OK then... we will do some hard math
     instead!';
10       var smallest=6;
11       var biggest=13;
12   } // end of the if else statement
13   var message = 'The game ends after five correct answers.';
14   ui.alert(title, message,ui.ButtonSet.OK);
15   }
```

Read this to understand what is going on in the code above.

3   We are going to start our Test function by setting response2 to the YES button. We can change this to ui.Button.NO to test the second part of the `if else` statement.

4-7   If the response is YES (which it will be because we set it to be on the first line!) then the title of the prompt is *Clever! Now you get to do the easy math.* We then set the value of two variables, smallest and biggest. These two numbers will determine how hard our multiplication problems will be, as we see in the next step.

8-11   If the user responds NO then the title is : *'OK then... we will do some hard math instead!'.* This part of the code can only run if we change the first line to: var response2 = ui.Button.NO;

13   We set a variable called message, that will show the same message to all players, whether they answered YES or NO to the question about easy multiplication.

14   Finally, we show the player an alert. The title of the alert will change, depending on what the value of reponse2 is (which is determined by whether the player answered YES or NO to the previous question). Because the player can only click OK we are <u>not</u> going to store the player's response in a variable.

28

Test it

Save your code, go back to your Google sheet and from the Math Game menu click Test Code. You should see the alert with the easy math message.

Change the first line of your Test function to this:

```
var response2 = ui.Button.NO;
```

Try it again

Save your code, go back to your Google sheet and click Test Code. You should see the alert with the hard math message.

Copy the new bit of code to your Main function

Now that you have the code for Step 3 working, copy it into your Main function. You don't need to copy the first three lines.

Your Main function should look like this:

```
function Main(){
// Step 1:
 var ui = SpreadsheetApp.getUi();
 var response = ui.prompt('Please enter your name.', ui.ButtonSet.OK);
 var student = response.getResponseText();

// Step 2:
var response2 = ui.alert( 'Hi '+ student +
'! Would you like to do some easy multiplication?',
ui.ButtonSet.YES_NO);

//Step 3:
if (response2== ui.Button.YES){
  var title= 'Clever! Now you get to do the easy math.';
  var smallest=1;
  var biggest=5;

} else {
  var title = 'OK then... we will do some hard math instead!';
  var smallest=6;
  var biggest=13;
} // end of the if else statement

var message = 'The game ends after five correct answers.';
ui.alert(title, message,ui.ButtonSet.OK);
}
```

Test your Main function

Save your code, go back to your Google sheet and this time click on Play Game from the Math Game menu. You should see the first three messages: one to ask you your name, a second to ask you if you would like to do some easy multiplication and a third telling you what kind of math you are going to do.

Clear out your Test function

Go back to your code screen and delete all the code in the Test function EXCEPT the first line:

```
var ui = SpreadsheetApp.getUi();
```

Why do we keep moving our code around?

Good question. We could just use the Main function and keep adding our code and not have a Test function at all. There are a few reasons we are using two functions in this project. Firstly, it is good practice to get in the habit of testing small chucks of code. This reduces the amount of time you need to spend finding bugs! Secondly, it helps you to recognise that the functions are encased in the braces { } and that it is important to keep the code from one function within the braces. Copying and pasting code is something that real programmers need to do quite a lot, and it is a good skill to pick up.

SUMMARY

You have written the code to do the first three steps of your math program. At this point, all of the code for the first three steps is in your Main function. Your Test function is almost empty, we just have the one line that gives us access to the user interface. We are ready to start coding Step 4 into our Test function.

Code for Math Game Step 4

In the next part of the program we need to ask the player multiplication questions until they answer five correctly.

We don't want to have to think up a whole list of multiplication questions, so we are going to have the computer randomly pick the numbers to multiply together. The numbers that we choose from will depend on whether the player gets hard problems or easy problems.

We already decided on the numbers to choose from in Step 3. The smallest number that we can pick from we called `smallest`, and the largest number that we can pick from we called `biggest`.

To pick a random number between our smallest and biggest numbers we are going to write a special function that we will call `randBetween`.

Random Numbers

Random numbers are fantastically useful for coding games. They allow you to introduce the element of surprise.

We won`t go into detail right now, but this function will pick out a number between two numbers and can include those numbers. If you are curious about how this works it is explained in the Appendix. For now, just type it into your Code.gs script and we can start using it.

Type this at the very bottom of your Code.gs script

This needs to go after the very last closing brace } of your Main function

```
// A custom function to pick a number between two numbers
function randBetween(min, max){
  var range = (max - min) + 1;
  return Math.floor((Math.random() * range) + min);
}
```

We will start by asking the user a single multiplication problem.

We want to present the player with something like this:

```
┌──────────────────────────────────────────┐
│                                        ✕   │
│   What is                                  │
│                                            │
│   2 x 1                                    │
│   ┌──────────────────────────────────┐    │
│   └──────────────────────────────────┘    │
│                                            │
│   ┌─────────────┐                          │
│   │     Ok      │                          │
│   └─────────────┘                          │
│                                            │
└──────────────────────────────────────────┘
```

We will use a prompt, because we want to provide a textbox for the answer and we will use the OK button.

Our prompt Title will be 'What is', and we will randomly select two numbers and put these two numbers into the message part of our prompt, along with the letter 'x', because it looks like a multiplication sign.

Looking back at our page on variables we can see that to make our message look like a multiplication problem we can join our numbers together with the 'x' like strings.

How to make our message look like a multiplication problem

If we have two numbers, stored in variables called `number1` and `number2` then we can join them together with the letter 'x' like this:
`number1 + 'x' + number2`

But – that would look something like this: **2x3**

 If we want to add a bit of space, to make the problem a little easier to read then we need to add the spaces in. We can do this by adding spaces around the letter x like this:
`number1 + ' x ' + number2`

This is how we are going to make the message part of our prompt.

Type this code into your Test function.

```
1    function Test(){
2    var ui = SpeadsheetApp.getUI();
3    var smallest = 1;
4    var biggest = 6;
5    var number1 = randBetween(smallest, biggest);
6    var number2 = randBetween(smallest, biggest);
7    var question = number1 + ' x ' + number2;
8    var response3 = ui.prompt('What is', question,
     ui.ButtonSet.OK);
9    var studentAnswer = response3.getResponseText();
10   }
```

Here's what's happening in each line of code.

1   This should already be in your script. It defines the start of the Test function

2   Because we copied this into the Main function we need to put it back to show the player alerts and prompts

3   This is the smallest number that will appear in the multiplication problem.

4   This is the biggest number.

5   This picks a number between smallest and biggest and stores it in the variable number1.

6   This picks another number and stores it in the variable number2.

7   This creates a *string* variable called question that will look something like this: 2 x 3

8   This shows the player a prompt with a title and the math question and the OK button and stores the player's answer in the response3 variable.

9   This puts what the player typed in the box into the studentAnswer variable.

10   We always need to end a function with a brace!

Test it

Save your code, go into your Google sheet and click on Test Code in the Math Game menu. You should be asked an easy multiplication question.

We're getting there... Now we need to keep asking questions until the user gets five correct answers.

Doing something repeatedly until something happens is a job for the While statement.

While statement

The `while` statement, like the `if else` statement checks to see if something is true.

It looks like this:

```
while (something){
      // repeat this code as long as something is true
}
```

We want to ask questions while the number of correct answers is less than five. As soon as the player has five correct answers we want to move on to Step 5.

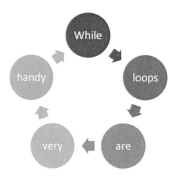

Our while condition will look like this:

```
while (correctAnswers < 5 ) {
// ask questions
}
```

We need a variable that keeps track of the number of correct questions - but first we need to figure out if the player answered the question correctly.

Keep track of the player's correct answers

Add in the code that is **in bold** below

```
function Test(){
var ui = SpeadsheetApp.getUI();
var smallest = 1;
var biggest = 6;
var correctAnswers = 0;                        Add This
var number1 = randBetween(smallest, biggest);
var number2 = randBetween(smallest, biggest);
var question = number1 + ' x ' + number2;
var response3 = ui.prompt('What is', question, ui.ButtonSet.OK);
var studentAnswer = response3.getResponseText();

var answer = number1*number2 ;
if (studentAnswer == answer) {                 And These Lines
     correctAnswer += 1;       // This adds 1
} // This is the end of the if statement

}
```

Where do we put the While loop?

We want to pick new numbers for each question, and if the user gets the question right we want to add 1 to the value of correctAnswer, but we don't want to set the value of correctAnswers to 0 each question - because then our loop would never end.

Take a moment and see if you can figure out where to put the while loop.

Add in the While loop

Add in the code that is **in bold** below

```
function Test(){
var ui = SpeadsheetApp.getUI();
var smallest = 1;
var biggest = 6;
var correctAnswers = 0;

while (correctAnswers<5){                          Add This
var number1 = randBetween(smallest, biggest);
var number2 = randBetween(smallest, biggest);
var question = number1 + ' x ' + number2;
var response3 = ui.prompt('What is', question, ui.ButtonSet.OK);
var studentAnswer = response3.getResponseText();

var answer = number1*number2 ;
if (studentAnswer == answer) {
      correctAnswers += 1;
}     // This ends the if statement
}     // This ends the while loop                  And This
} // This ends the function
```

Test it out!

Go back to your Google Sheet and run Test Code in the Math Game menu. You should be presented with easy multiplication questions until you answer five correctly.

Before we move on to the last part of our program we are going to learn a bit about working with numbers.

Working with numbers

Here are some of the things you can do with numeric variables (numbers) in Javascript.

Increment a number ++ or +=

```
myNumber = 1;          sets the value of myNumber to 1
myNumber ++;           adds 1 to myNumber
myNumber +=2;          adds 2 to myNumber
```

Decrement a number -- or -=

```
myNumber = 5;          sets the value of myNumber to 5
myNumber --;           substracts 1 from myNumber
myNumber -=2;          subtracts 2 from myNumber
```

Adding & Subtracting

```
2 + 5;        equals 7
5 - 3;        equals 2
```

Multiplying & Dividing

```
2 * 5;        equals 10
10/5;         equals 2
```

Modulus Division - the division remainder

```
10%3;         equals 1
```

Order of Operations

Javascript follows order of operation conventions. **B**rackets are evaluated first, the **e**xponents, followed by **m**ultiplication and **d**ivision and then **a**ddition and **s**ubtraction. A good way to remember this is **BEDMAS.**

Code for Math Game Step 5

Now we want to show the player a message that the game is over and how many questions it took to answer five questions correctly.

Hmmm..

We have a little problem - we didn't keep track of how many questions we asked in total.

Think about how we could do this.

We need a new variable that we will call questionsAsked and the handy increment operator +=.

Keep track of the total number of questions asked

Add in the code that is **in bold** below

```
function Test(){
var ui = SpeadsheetApp.getUI();
var smallest = 1;
var biggest = 6;
var correctAnswers = 0;
var questionsAsked = 0;        Add This
while (correctAnswers<5){
var number1 = randBetween(smallest, biggest);
var number2 = randBetween(smallest, biggest);
var question = number1 + ' x ' + number2;
var response = ui.prompt('What is', question, ui.ButtonSet.OK);
var studentAnswer = response.getResponseText();

questionsAsked+=1;              And This

var answer = number1*number2 ;
if (studentAnswer == answer) {
     correctAnswers += 1;
}       This brace ends the if statement
}              This brace ends the while statement
}                    This brace ends the function
```

We are ready to show the player the last message

Here's what the final message should look like:

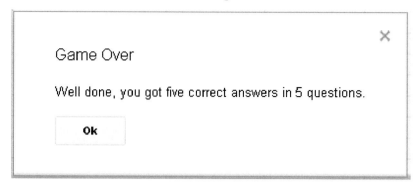

We know how to do this.

We show an alert, because we don't need a textbox. We show the OK button. We show both a Title and a Message. Lastly, we don't need to store the user's response because the game is over!

We are going to use two lines of code; one to put the message together and one to show the alert.

Add these two lines of code to the end of the Test function

```
var message = 'Well done, you got five correct answers in ' +
questionsAsked + ' questions.';
ui.alert('Game Over', message, ui.ButtonSet.OK);
```

Test it

Go back to your Google Sheet and run Test Code from the Math Game menu.

Voila! That's all the coding done.

Now you just need to put it all together.

Copy this code from your Test function to your Main function:

This code goes at the end of the Main function, *before* the closing brace **}**

```
var correctAnswers = 0;
var questionsAsked = 0;
while (correctAnswers<5){
var number1 = randBetween(smallest, biggest);
var number2 = randBetween(smallest, biggest);
var question = number1 + ' x ' + number2;
var response3 = ui.prompt('What is', question,
ui.ButtonSet.OK);
var studentAnswer = response3.getResponseText();

questionsAsked+=1;

var answer = number1*number2 ;
if (studentAnswer == answer) {
     correctAnswers += 1;
}
}
var message = 'Well done, you got five correct answers in ' +
questionsAsked + ' questions.';
ui.alert('Game Over', message, ui.ButtonSet.OK);
```

You did it!

Go to your Google Sheet and run Play Game from the Math Game menu.
You've just written an interactive game using Google App Script.

Congratulations!

Now what?

You've learned a lot from this short program. Now you should be able to:
1. Show the player a message and get information from the player
2. Use the if statement
3. Use the while loop to repeat parts of your code
4. Do simple things with variables, like joining words together and adding numbers.

Try changing your game

Change the game –can you randomly pick a number between 1 and 10 and count how many tries it takes for the player to guess the number? What other games can you come up with?

Where to go from here

We have only scratched the surface of all the great things you can do with Javascript and Google App Script.

There are lots and lots of great resources on the web so help you learn coding. To find out more about Javascript visit http://www.w3schools.com/js/

Code Academy is a fantastic website that will help you learn coding in lots of great languages: http://www.codecademy.com/

Try out some other projects:

You can learn more about coding with Google App Script at the website for this book: https://sites.google.com/site/gascoding/
There are a couple of other fun projects there that will expand your coding abilities and are fun to use. There is an encryption script so that you can send your friends secret messages and there is an automatic essay writer, in case you don't feel like writing one yourself!

To use these projects, copy the code just like you did for this project. Then run the code from the new menu. Play around with the code and see if you can make the programs better – can you program the computer to write a whole story? These extra projects are commented, but if anything doesn't make sense look on the w3schools website, it can teach you about all the different things you can do with Javascript.

Have fun!

Appendix

randBetween function

This is a very useful function that randomly selects a number between min and max, inclusive. That means that it can pick any number between min and max, but it could also pick min or max. The basis of this function are two Javascript functions found in the Math library: floor and random.

Math.random() generates a random number between 0 and 1, but not including 1. To get a random number greater than 1, we need to multiply our random number by our required *range.* The range is the spread of numbers - so if we want numbers between 2 and 5 (including 2 and 5) then that is a range of four numbers (2,3,4 and 5).

We calculate our range as: max - min +1 when we want to be able to pick from our min and our max.

Math.random() * range will give us a number between 0 and range

Math.random() * range +min will give us a number between min and max.

This function takes two *arguments* – min and max. Function arguments are placed in the brackets immediately after the function name. These same argument names don't need to be used when you call the function in your program, but they do need to appear in the function itself.

```
function randBetween(min, max){
  var range = (max - min) + 1;
  return Math.floor((Math.random() * range) + min);
}
```

To pick a number between 6 and 16 you would type: randBetween(6,16).

If you wanted to store this number in a variable called goodNumber you would type:
var goodNumber = randBetween(6,16);

47174894R00025

Made in the USA
San Bernardino, CA
23 March 2017